D0633821

NO LONGER
PROPERTY OF PPLD

Selena Gomez

ABDO
Publishing Company

A Big Buddy Book
by **Sarah Tieck**

VISIT US AT
www.abdopublishing.com

Published by ABDO Publishing Company, 8000 West 78th Street, Edina, Minnesota 55439.

Copyright © 2009 by Abdo Consulting Group, Inc. International copyrights reserved in all countries. No part of this book may be reproduced in any form without written permission from the publisher. Buddy Books™ is a trademark and logo of ABDO Publishing Company.

Printed in the United States of America, North Mankato, Minnesota.
122009 032011

Coordinating Series Editor: Rochelle Baltzer
Contributing Editor: Marcia Zappa
Graphic Design: Maria Hosley
Cover Photograph: *AP Photo*: Chris Pizzello
Interior Photographs/Illustrations: *AP Photo*: Tammie Arroyo (p. 21), George Gongora-Corpus Christi Caller-Times
    (p. 7), Jennifer Graylock (p. 18), Graylock.com (pp. 7, 20), Reinhold Matay (p. 17), Donna McWilliam (p. 15),
    Denis Poroy (p. 24), Dan Steinberg (p. 27); *Clipart.com* (p. 9); *FilmMagic*: Jean-Paul Aussenard/WireImage
    (p. 23); *Getty Images*: Jean-Paul Aussenard/WireImage (p. 10), Toby Canham (p. 5), F. Micelotta/American Idol
    2008/Getty Images for Fox (p. 25), Mark Peristein (p. 13), John Shearer (p. 28); *iStockPhoto*: Paul Fleet (p. 9),
    Photomorphic (p. 9), Robert Plotz (p. 9).

Library of Congress Cataloging-in-Publication Data

Tieck, Sarah, 1976-
  Selena Gomez / Sarah Tieck.
    p. cm. -- (Big buddy biographies)
  ISBN 978-1-60453-548-8
  1. Gomez, Selena, 1992---Juvenile literature. 2. Actors--United States--Biography--Juvenile literature. 3. Singers--United States--Biography--Juvenile literature. I. Title.

PN2287.G585T54 2009
791.4302'8092--dc22
[B]
                                    2008033517

Selena
Gomez

Contents

Rising Star

Selena Gomez is an actress and a singer. She has appeared in television shows and movies. Selena is known for starring in *Wizards of Waverly Place*.

Selena plays Alex Russo in *Wizards of Waverly Place.*

Family Ties

Selena Gomez was born on July 22, 1992. She has lived most of her life in Grand Prairie, Texas.

Selena's parents are Mandy Teefey and Ricardo Gomez. Selena also has a stepfather, Brian Teefey. She has no brothers or sisters.

Did you know...

Selena's family is Mexican and Italian. Selena values her background.

Selena is named for a famous Mexican-American singer, Selena Quintanilla Pérez.

Growing Up

When Selena was five, Mandy and Ricardo parted. Selena stayed with her mom. She was raised in Grand Prairie, Texas. Grand Prairie is located near Dallas.

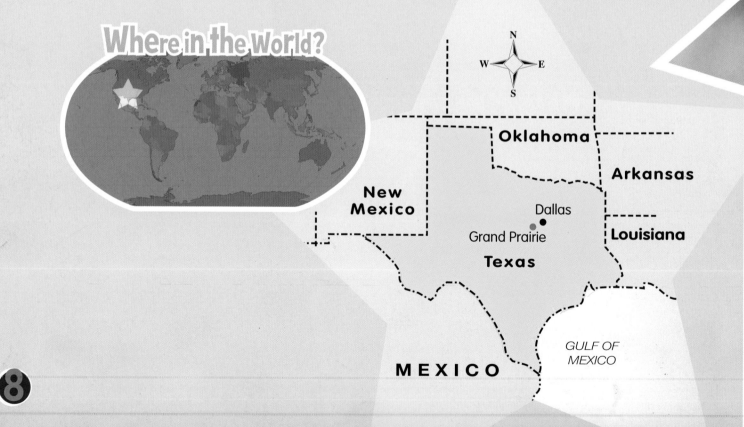

Where in the World?

Oklahoma

Arkansas

New Mexico

Dallas

Grand Prairie

Louisiana

Texas

MEXICO

GULF OF MEXICO

When people think of Texas, they often think of cowboys (*left*), oil wells (*center*), and barbecued food (*right*).

Dallas is the third-largest city in Texas. It is home to the Dallas Cowboys football team.

Selena met actress Demi Lovato at tryouts for *Barney and Friends*. They became friends right away, and they are still close.

Did you know...
Barney and Friends was Selena's first audition.

A Young Actress

When Selena was growing up, her mother was an actress. Soon, Selena also wanted to be an actress. So, she **auditioned** for *Barney and Friends*. She was excited when she got a **role**! Selena would play a girl named Gianna.

Did you know...

In 1988, *Barney and Friends* started as a video series called *Barney and the Backyard Gang*. The television show debuted in 1992.

Lights! Camera! Action!

Selena became a **professional** actress when she began to appear regularly on *Barney and Friends*. *Barney and Friends* is a popular television show for young children.

Barney is a large purple dinosaur. His world is full of music, games, and fun.

Did you know...

Demi Lovato was also an actress on *Barney and Friends*. She played a girl named Angela.

Selena appeared on *Barney and Friends* for about two years. On the **set**, Selena improved her acting and singing skills. She learned how to work with the camera. Working as an actress helped her become less shy.

Barney and Friends has made more than ten seasons of shows! There are many Barney movies, too.

Did you know...

Because of her work, Selena does not attend a regular school. She learns from private teachers at home. This is called homeschooling. Selena enjoys studying science.

Discovered

When Selena was about 12 years old, Disney was holding a search for talented performers. Selena decided to audition.

Disney liked Selena's acting and singing and wanted her to work for them. They wanted to find the right role for Selena. So, they asked her to do more tryouts.

Selena was part of the 2008 Disney Channel Games. Each year at the games, Disney stars compete in activities such as relay races.

Dylan (*left*) and Cole (*right*) Sprouse are twins. They star in *The Suite Life of Zack & Cody.*

Miley Cyrus is the star of *Hannah Montana.*

In 2006 and 2007, Selena had small **roles** on popular shows. She played Gwen on *The Suite Life of Zack & Cody* and Mikayla on *Hannah Montana.* For a while, she and her mother traveled to Los Angeles, California, for her work. Finally, they moved there so Selena could be close to work.

Big Break

Soon, Selena got a starring **role** on a new Disney show. She would play a girl named Alex Russo. In 2007, *Wizards of Waverly Place* **debuted**.

Twice before, Selena had gotten starring roles in television shows. But they never **aired**. So, *Wizards of Waverly Place* was an important step for Selena.

Selena and her character, Alex, like the same fashions. They both love sneakers!

Jake T. Austin, Selena, David Henrie, and David DeLuise (*left to right*) work together on *Wizards of Waverly Place*.

Wizards of Waverly Place

Wizards of Waverly Place is a popular show on the Disney Channel. Almost 6 million people watched the first **episode**!

The show takes place in New York City, New York. In the show, Alex Russo and her two brothers have magical powers. They learn spells from their father.

Selena is becoming more well-known. Sometimes fans ask for an autograph or a picture.

> Drew Seeley sang with Vanessa Hudgens in High School Musical: The Concert. He also wrote and sang songs for the movie *High School Musical*.

Movies and Music

In addition to television work, Selena appears in movies. In 2008's *Horton Hears a Who!*, she provided the voice of Helga. And, she starred with Drew Seeley in *Another Cinderella Story*.

In *Horton Hears a Who!*, Selena worked with funny actor Jim Carrey. Jim provided the voice for an elephant named Horton. He dressed up like Horton to tell people about the movie.

Like Selena, Nick, Joe, and Kevin Jonas are well-known young stars. They are members of a band called Jonas Brothers.

Selena has also made her mark in music. She sang the opening song for *Wizards of Waverly Place*. She sang and danced in *Another Cinderella Story*, too. And in 2008, Selena appeared in Jonas Brothers' "Burnin' Up" music video.

Did you know...

Selena learned tango for *Another Cinderella Story*. Tango is a style of ballroom dance that has Hispanic roots.

27

Selena supports causes that are important to her. In 2008, she attended an event that helped raise money for sick children.

Did you know...

Selena has been a guest on radio and television shows. In 2008, she appeared on *The Ellen DeGeneres Show*.

Buzz

Selena continues to work as an actress. In 2008, she started working with Demi Lovato on the movie *Princess Protection Program*.

Selena would like to use her singing talent to start a band. Many believe Selena Gomez has a bright **future**.

Snapshot

★ **Name**: Selena Gomez

★ **Birthday**: July 22, 1992

★ **Raised in**: Grand Prairie, Texas

★ **Appearances**: *Barney and Friends, Wizards of Waverly Place, Horton Hears a Who!, Another Cinderella Story, Princess Protection Program*

Important Words

air to show on television or play on the radio.

audition (aw-DIH-shuhn) to give a trial performance showcasing personal talent as a musician, a singer, a dancer, or an actor.

debut (DAY-byoo) to make a first appearance.

episode one show in a series of shows.

future (FYOO-chuhr) a time that has not yet occurred.

professional (pruh-FEHSH-nuhl) working for money rather than for pleasure.

role a part an actor plays in a show.

set the place where a movie or a television show is recorded.

Web Sites

To learn more about Selena Gomez, visit ABDO Publishing Company online. Web sites about Selena Gomez are featured on our Book Links page. These links are routinely monitored and updated to provide the most current information available.

www.abdopublishing.com

Index